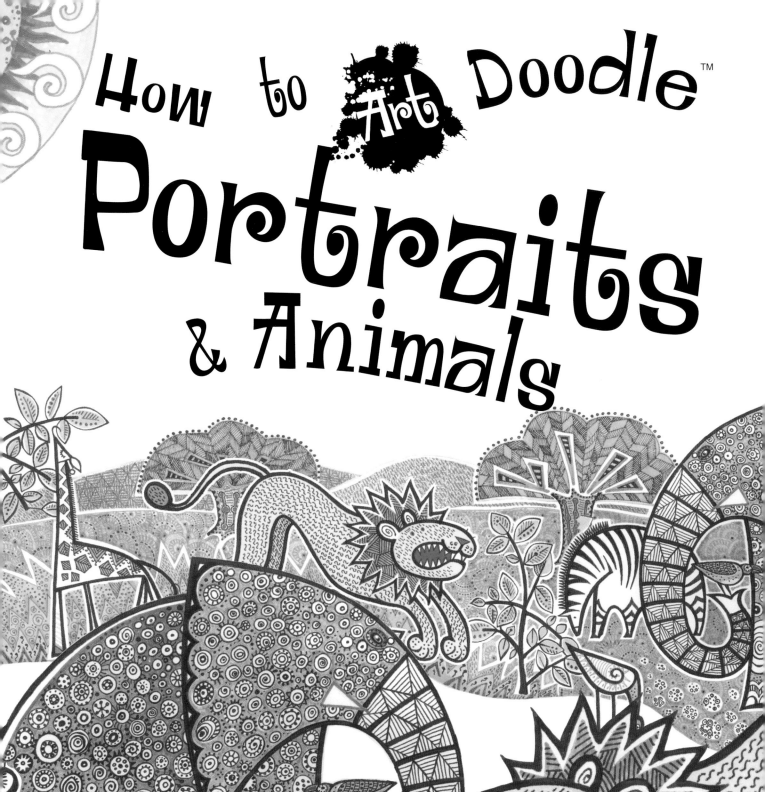

How to Art Doodle™

Portraits

& Animals

Carolyn Scrace

This edition first published in MMXV by
Book House

Distributed by Black Rabbit Books
P.O. Box 3263
Mankato
Minnesota MN 56002

© MMXV The Salariya Book Company Ltd
Printed in the United States of America.
Printed on paper from sustainable forests.

Cataloging-in-Publication Data is available
from the Library of Congress

HB ISBN: 978-1-909645-49-3
PB ISBN: 978-1-910184-37-0

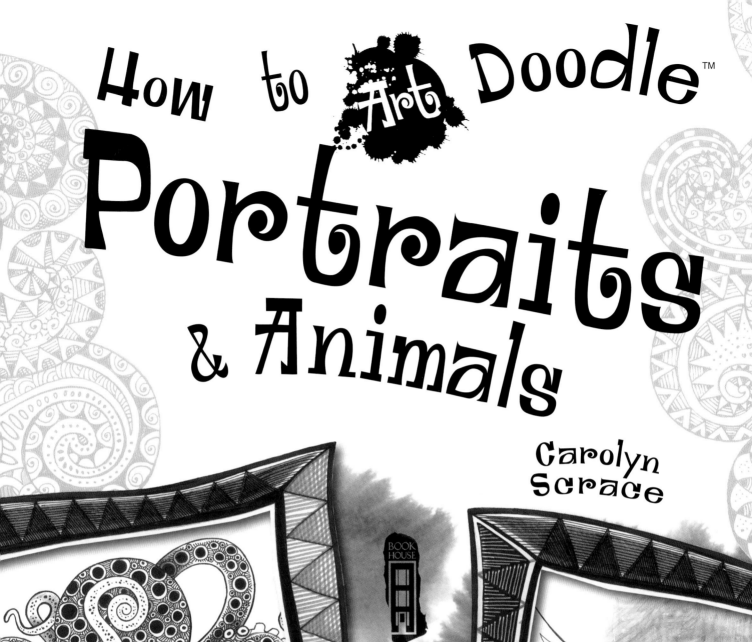

How to Art Doodle™

Portraits
& Animals

Carolyn Scrace

BOOK HOUSE

Contents

Please note: Sharp blades and scissors should be used under adult supervision.

Introduction

A rt Doodling releases creativity and develops drawing skills. Discover the thrill of using simple Art Doodle patterns to build up a complex picture. These pages are packed with inspirational ideas and designs that show how easily amazing effects can be achieved.

Do it anywhere!

Art Doodling can be done anywhere, and needs no special equipment! Some of the best Art Doodles are often drawn on the back of receipts or paper towels!

Inspiration

Inspiration is all around you; as you walk in the park, daydream on the bus—even as you eat your breakfast! Before long you will see ideas for Art Doodle patterns and compositions everywhere—even in the most suprising places!

Sketchbook

Keep a small sketchbook or notepad with you at all times! Use it for creative Art Doodling and to jot down ideas. Stick in any inspiring magazine cuttings you find, and remember to use it as a work in progress!

Art Doodling

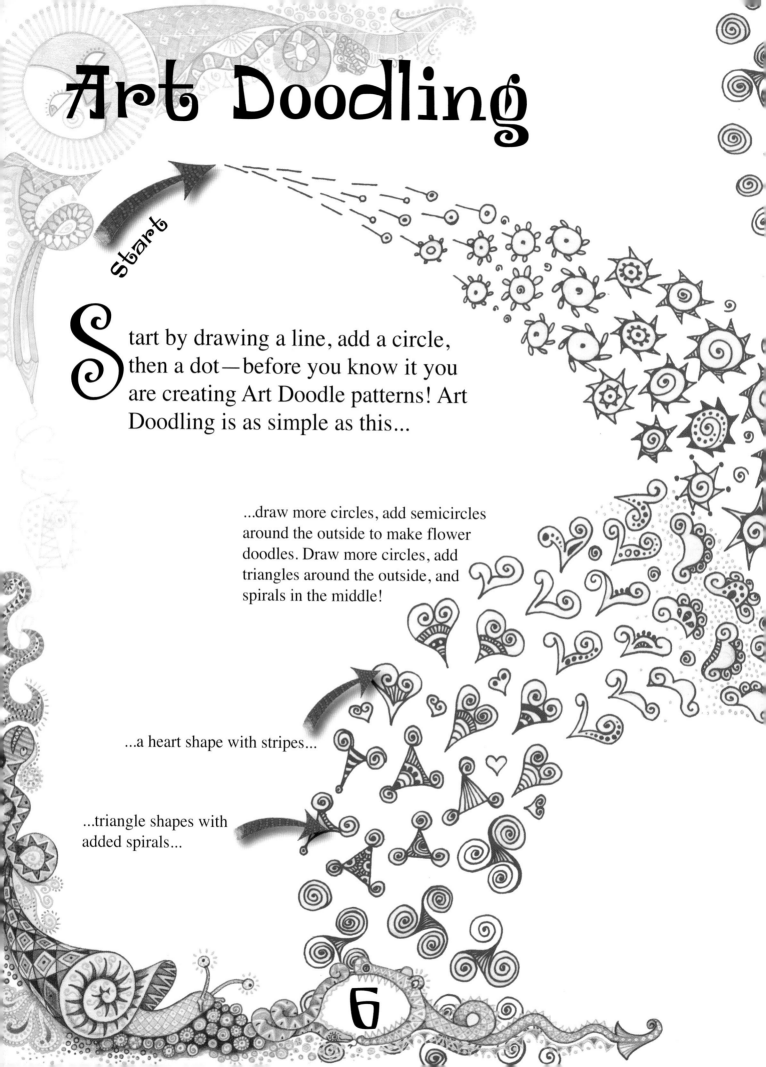

start

Start by drawing a line, add a circle, then a dot—before you know it you are creating Art Doodle patterns! Art Doodling is as simple as this...

...draw more circles, add semicircles around the outside to make flower doodles. Draw more circles, add triangles around the outside, and spirals in the middle!

...a heart shape with stripes...

...triangle shapes with added spirals...

6

Creating these patterns will
enable you to Art Doodle some
of these wonderful patterned
swirls (right).

7

Pencil sharpener

Eraser

Graphite pencils come in different grades, from hard to soft. The softer the pencil, the darker the mark it makes.

Thick **marker pens** are perfect for filling in large areas. Fine **permanent marker** pens are great for outlines and details.

Tools & materials

There are no special tools and materials needed for Art Doodling. An old pencil stub and a scrap of paper are all you need to get started! You may, however, wish to use some or all of the tools and materials suggested here. It's important to experiment and try to use whatever tools and materials inspire and excite you.

Pencil crayons are ideal for adding soft shading and for coloring in.

Thick **felt-tip pens** are ideal for blocking-in large areas of color.

Fineliner pens produce a flowing line. They come in a wide range of colors and are ideal for intricate doodling.

A **black gel pen** is useful for outlines and detailed doodles. **Metallic and white gel pens** are ideal for doodling onto colored paper or over dark-colored Art Doodles.

8

Double-sided tape

Sketchbook for jotting down ideas and trying out designs.

Use your sketchbook for experimenting with new techniques, and keep notes of what materials you used.

Types of paper

Cartridge paper comes in a variety of weights. Heavyweight paper is good for water-based paint. Note: Ink lines may bleed on some cartridge papers.

Bristol board or **paper** may be textured or smooth. Smooth Bristol board is good to work on with pencils, pencil crayons, markers, felt-tips, and gel and fineliner pens for adding fine details.

Gouache is opaque paint. Use it for painting plain, flat areas.

Colored inks and **watercolor** paints are ideal for covering large areas of a design with subtle color.

Paintbrushes come in a wide range of sizes.

Palette (or clean saucer) for mixing paint.

Art Doodle face

Drawing faces realistically can be extremely difficult, but a simple graphic style can easily be achieved. All faces can be broken down into basic shapes as in these diagrams below.

1. Draw an oval shape with a vertical line through the center.

2. Draw in the eyeline—a horizontal line through the center. Add a line for the nose.

3. Draw in the eyes and nose. Add eyebrows then draw in the mouth.

1. Using scrap paper, sketch in a head, and face. Merge the top of the head into a peacock shape. Add a crazy, curly hairdo.

2. Trace the design onto cartridge paper and Art Doodle into it. Use a limited palette of colors: red, ochre, and fuschia.

Photograph

Art Doodling a photograph of someone is great fun. Personalize their Art Doodled portrait by incorporating patterns that characterize their personality or interests.

1. Black and white photographs can be particularly effective for Art Doodling. Photocopy your photograph to experiment with your design.

2. Trace the main shapes onto paper. Draw a curved line through the center. Cut out one side of the head and stick it onto the photocopy. Now repeat with the shoulder and background of the opposite side.

3. This person's main interests of photography, film-making, and music form the basis of the patterns. Use this version to test what works—the doodling on the face is not used in the final design.

4. Stick the photograph onto a sheet of cartridge paper. Trace your design onto thinner cartridge paper and cut out the shapes you want to Art Doodle. Stick them in place. Use a marker pen to fill in big areas of black. Start Art Doodling!

5. Add a bold picture frame to finish the composition.

Doodled mermaid

Mermaids appear in the mythology of different countries and cultures all over the world. Half woman, half fish, they make a wonderful starting point for freeing your imagination when designing an Art Doodle.

1. Start with a thumbnail sketch on scrap paper. Include as many sea creatures as possible in the composition: fish, shells, and seahorses. The curving tentacles of the octopus "hairdo" make fantastic shapes for Art Doodling.

2. Once you are happy with your design, draw the final, enlarged version onto cartridge paper. Now start Art Doodling! Fill in the background shape with black marker pen to create dramatic contrast.

Art Doodle owl

Throughout the ages owls have fascinated mankind. In some cultures owls symbolize wisdom, while in others they herald doom or even death.

1. Start with a rough sketch of an owl. Make its eyes the focal point of the drawing. The owl's feathers make great shapes for Art Doodle patterns.

2. To create this background you need cartridge paper, a broad paintbrush, and watercolor paints. Use criss-crossing brush strokes to overlap the colors.

3. Draw the owl onto a sheet of cartridge paper. Make it slightly bigger than the textured background. Start doodling!

4. Cut out the owl and stick it onto the textured background. Finish doodling the owl's body in black, white, and gray. Restrict color to the focal points: the eyes, ears, and beak.

5. Color in the eyes with blue and yellow felt-tip pens, leaving white highlights. Go over the blue pupils with black pencil crayon. Add layers of orange and red pencil crayoning to the yellow pupils to strengthen the colors.

6. Add pencil shading to the doodles to create a sense of depth.

Art Doodle lion

Throughout art history images of lions have been used as potent symbols. They are depicted as powerful creatures that can also be gentle at the same time. The image of the "king of the jungle" symbolizes stateliness and bravery.

1. Make a rough thumbnail sketch. Keep the shapes large and bold to Art Doodle. Draw the lion's face as a series of circles.

2. Draw an enlarged version of your design onto cartridge paper. Pencil in vertical and horizontal lines to help with symmetry and balance.

3. Start Art Doodling. Create an effective design touch by only coloring selected parts of the picture. This makes the lion's face into a dramatic focal point.

4. Adding pencil shading around the lion's face gives it a subtle three-dimensional quality that makes it stand out against the mane.

safari animals

Art doodling drawings of animals in their natural environment is terrific fun. Draw some of your favorite African safari animals, add acacia trees, a watering hole, grassland, and then Art Doodles.

1. Lightly sketch your composition on scrap paper. Try a landscape format for a change. Stylizing the shape of the animals is an effective approach for Art Doodles. Keep the background simple.

20

2. Draw your design onto cartridge paper. Use a thick, felt-tip pen to outline the animals. Start blocking in areas of color.

3. Leave a white line around each of the main shapes to make them stand out against the background. Then start Art Doodling!

21

Pattern builder

These step-by-step examples show how to Art Doodle some of the patterns used in this book.

Art Doodle face (pages 10-11)

1. Pencil in a triangle shape as a guide. Use black fineliner or gel pens to draw in the bird's head. Add rows of scallop shapes.

2. Add more rows of scallop shapes.

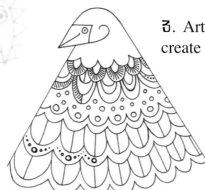

3. Art Doodle lines to create feather patterns.

4. Color in some areas with black felt-tip pen to add contrast.

Art Doodle owl (pages 16-17)

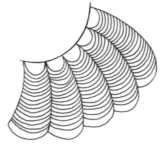

1. Draw scallop shapes around the owl's eye.

2. Draw in a series of curves as shown.

3. Add rows of scallop shapes.

4. Finish off the doodles. Add pencil shading.

Glossary

Background   area behind an object or image.

Blocking-in   where areas of flat color are put down.

Composition   how an artist arranges shapes, sizes, and colors, the different elements that make a piece of art.

Design   a graphic representation, usually a drawing or a sketch.

Focal point   the center of interest in a work of art.

Highlights   small, brightly lit areas on a painting.

Landscape format   a design format where the width is larger than the height.

Light source   the direction of light.

Limited palette   when an artist restricts the number of colors used.

Proportion   the size, location, or amount of one part of an image in relation to another.

Rough (rough sketch)   a quick sketch of the main elements in a picture.

Shading   the lines or marks used to fill in areas or represent gradations of color or tone.

Sketch   a preparatory drawing.

Stylize   depict or treat in nonrealistic style.

Symbolism   the use of symbols to express or represent ideas.

Symmetrical   formed by similar parts, either facing or around an axis.

Technique   an accepted method used to produce something.

Tentacles   the long, flexible arms of animals (such as an octopus).

Three-dimensional   having, or appearing to have, the dimension of depth as well as width and height.

Thumbnail (sketches)   usually very small, quick, abbreviated drawings.

23

Index